ABUNDANT TRUTH INTERNATIONAL MINISTRIES

C.O.G.I.C. Protocols Series

THE MISSION OF THE DEACON

Practical Guidelines for Aspirant C.O.G.I.C. Deacons

Roderick Levi Evans

The Mission of the Deacon
Practical Guidelines for Aspirant C.O.G.I.C. Deacons

All Rights Reserved ©2025 by Roderick L. Evans

No part of this book may be reproduced or transmitted in any form or by any means, graphic, electronic, or mechanical, including photocopying, recording, taping, or by any information storage or retrieval system, without the permission in writing from the publisher.

Front & Back Cover Designs by
Abundant Truth Publishing, U.S.A. All rights reserved

Abundant Truth Publishing
an imprint of Abundant Truth International Ministries

For information address:
Abundant Truth International
P.O. Box 126
Camden, NC 27921

Unless otherwise indicated, all of the scripture quotations are taken from the *Authorized King James Version* of the Bible. Scripture quotations marked with NIV are taken from the *New International Version* of the Bible. Scripture quotations marked with NASV are taken from the *New American Standard Version* of the Bible. Scripture quotations marked with Amplified are taken from the *Amplified Bible.*

ISBN 13: 9798294027926

Printed in the United States of America

Contents

Introduction

Prologue: The C.O.G.I.C. Deacon   1

The Model of Service   3
The Purpose of Preparation   4

Section 1 – The Quest for Servants   5
Servants

The Original Problem   12
The Original Proposition   17
The Original Procedure   21

Section 2 – The Qualifications of   31
of Servants

Qualification of Honest Report   35

Contents (cont.)

Qualification of Full of the Holy Ghost   41
Qualification of full of Wisdom   47

Section 3 – The Quality of Service   57

Mortification of Murmuring   60
Magnification of the Word   64
Multiplication of Disciples   68

Section 4 – The Office of the Deacon   77

The Deacon's Character   81
The Deacon's Charge   90

Section 5 – The Deacon and the Church   101

The Deacon and the Pastor   104

Contents (cont.)

The Deacon and the Laity   109
The Deacon and the Deacons   113

Bibliography   **121**

Disclaimer: The information presented is not officially endoresed by the Church or any Jurisidiction, but provided as a supplement to the established order and protocols of C.O.G.I.C.

Introduction

The Church of God in Christ is an organization committed to Jesus Christ. It is known for its powerful minister and ministries. It is also known for being demonstrators of the verse which states "let all things be done decently and in order.

The C.O.G.I.C. Protocols Series was developed to aid ministers and those involved in the work of the Lord. It is our prayer that the materials presented will add to one's understanding of protocols and practices within the church. It is provided as supplemental information to the Official Manuals and Publications of the church.

In this publication:

The focus of this publication is to bring clarity and understanding to the deacon ministry. Deacons and servants are needed in the Church. The early Church recognized their importance and Paul wrote qualifications to this office.

Deacons are responsible for more than counting money and maintaining church property. Their office requires them also to be men of the Spirit. To bring understanding and clarity to this office, this book was written.

In this publication, we will examine

the history and subsequent development of the Deacon's office in the Church. In addition, we will learn how the first men who were appointed to serve in the Church are the standard for which deacons and servants are to evaluate their service today.

In doing so, the Church, deacons, and those called to serve will benefit from mutual understanding and cooperation. Consequently, a greater appreciation for this type of ministry will be developed.

Moreover, deacons who operate in the Church of God in Christ will be strengthened and encouraged to execute their duties in accordance with the standards set with in the Church as outlined in the Official Manual.

-Prologue-

The C.O.G.I.C. Deacon

THE MISSION OF THE DEACON

THE MISSION OF THE DEACON

The call to serve is an honor from God. Jesus said let the greatest among you be your servant.

The Model of Service

This is the foundation for the C.O.G.I.C. deacon.

> *But he that is greatest among you shall be your servant. (Matthew 23:11)*

Unlike other reformations where the deacons control the pastor and the operations of the Church, the C.O.G.I.C. deacon has the attitude of service.

The Purpose of Preparation

This study is designed to prepare those who want to accept an appointment as a deacon. It is not designed to give biblical guidelines for the spiritual requirements and perspectives of the aspirant deacon. This will aid the deacon as he follows the protocols of the church.

-Section 1-

The Quest for Servants

THE MISSION OF THE DEACON

Every member of the Body of Christ is called to serve. God places individuals in the Church as it pleases Him. In doing so, He defines how we are to serve and in what capacity. Jesus revealed the need for a servant's mentality in those who desired greatness in the kingdom.

> *But it shall not be so among you: but whosoever will be great among you, let him be your minister; And whosoever will be chief among you, let him be your servant: Even as the Son of man came not to be ministered unto, but to minister, and*

THE MISSION OF THE DEACON

to give his life a ransom for many. (Matthew 20:26-28)

In today's Church, we believe that those who serve in a particular ministry office or those who hold an ecclesiastical position are great. However, if an individual possesses an office or title and does not serve the people of God for their spiritual benefit and welfare, they have not fulfilled their responsibilities before the Lord.

Jesus stated that He was the standard for servant hood. He did not make personal and selfish demands upon

THE MISSION OF THE DEACON

those who followed Him. However, He came to serve their spiritual needs culminating in His ultimate sacrifice for all mankind. May all members in the Church remember His example!

God has set members in the Church as it has pleased Him. He is the one who calls, anoints, and appoints. As recipients of God's grace and spiritual endowment, we should respect one another for what capacity of service God has called each to function. God gives diversity as a tool whereby the members of Christ's Body are connected and interdependent on one another for overall spiritual success and growth.

In his first letter to the Corinthian church, Paul reminded the believers of God's purpose for gifts and ministries. At the end of his discourse in chapter 12, he gives some insight into how ministries and gifts were established within the Church.

> *And God hath set some in the church, first apostles, secondarily prophets, thirdly teachers, after that miracles, then gifts of healings, helps, governments, diversities of tongues. (I Corinthians 12:28)*

THE MISSION OF THE DEACON

After citing the foundational and teaching ministries, Paul reveals that the gifts of miracles and healings were set in the Church. Instead of God continuing with other 'power' gifts and ministries, we discover that the gift and/or ministry of helps were set in the Church.

Though all are called to serve, there are individuals who receive an endowment of the Spirit to serve in the Church.

Though in today's churches, many departments, auxiliaries, and groups have been created as avenues of service, the

THE MISSION OF THE DEACON

scriptures give us one example of a ministry whose sole purpose is to serve – the Deacon.

The Original Problem

The Book of Acts chronicles the beginning and expansion of the Church. After Peter's first sermon on the day of Pentecost, the Church grew exponentially.

> *And with many other words did he testify and exhort, saying, Save yourselves from this untoward generation. Then they that gladly received his word were baptized: and the same day there were added unto*

THE MISSION OF THE DEACON

them about three thousand souls. (Acts 2:40-41)

The healing of the man at the gate led to another multitude of people hearing the gospel, which increased the number of disciples further.

Howbeit many of them which heard the word believed; and the number of the men was about five thousand. (Acts 4:4)

From two sermons, the numbers of disciples grew by eight thousand, not mentioning the numerous conversions occurring daily. The early Church was characterized by charity and good works. Individuals sold possessions so that others would have their needs met.

The apostles preached, taught, and worked miracles while facilitating distribution of goods as well as taking care of food distribution. This became a problem and burden to their ministries.

As the number of disciples grew, the number of people with needs grew accordingly. The apostles became overwhelmed with trying to fast, pray, teach, work miracles, and handle the other needs of all the people. In turn, some did

THE MISSION OF THE DEACON

not get their needs met.

And in those days, when the number of the disciples was multiplied, there arose a murmuring of the Grecians against the Hebrews, because their widows were neglected in the daily ministration. (Acts 6:1)

Some of the widows were overlooked in the daily distribution, which led to complaint and division among the people. This leads us to some important points.

1)   As a church grows, the number and diversity of needs will multiply.

2) Complaining is a common response, even among Christians.

3) Church leaders are to be responsive to the valid needs of the people.

One unmet need in a church can lead to division among the people. The apostles recognized that they could not perform their duties as ministers of the gospel by doing what others could do.

This led to the appointment and ordination of individuals to a ministry of service. Remember you are called to service to meet a need.

THE MISSION OF THE DEACON

The Original Proposition

The apostles had to find a suitable solution to the incomplete daily food distribution. In response to this need, the apostles sent a proposition throughout the brethren.

This proposition would solve the current dissention among the people while freeing the apostles to concentrate on ministry.

Then the twelve called the multitude of the disciples unto them, and said, It is not reason that we should leave the word of God, and serve tables.

THE MISSION OF THE DEACON

Wherefore, brethren, look ye out among you seven men of honest report, full of the Holy Ghost and wisdom, whom we may appoint over this business. (Acts 6:2-3)

The proposition was simple; find individuals among the brethren who would be able to perform this duty. Though the need seemed minor, it required that men of spiritual distinction be placed in charge over it. This point deserves further discussion.

In the Church today, anyone who is willing is oftentimes placed in positions of service both great and small. However, the apostles demonstrated that anyone who serves in the Church should have spiritual wisdom and maturity regardless of the task; even if they are to serve food.

The call to serve is a call to be spiritually mature. Those who want to serve have to make sure that they are sound, solid, and spiritual Christians.

The proposition, again, served a two-fold purpose. The first was to quiet unrest among the widows. The second purpose was to liberate the apostles from this task

THE MISSION OF THE DEACON

to do the work of the ministry; which was the spreading of the gospel and establishing the believers in the faith.

> *But we will give ourselves continually to prayer, and to the ministry of the word. (Acts 6:4)*

Herein is the true goal of service in the Kingdom of God: People are placed in positions of service so that the work of Jesus Christ continues without hindrances.

With this in mind, it is easy to see why many pastors are overloaded because they are spending time fulfilling personal needs of the congregation, which could be performed by others.

The Original Procedure

After presenting their proposition, the apostles instituted the procedure to find suitable candidates for service.

Earlier, we stated how the Church from two sermons grew by eight thousand individuals. Thus, the number of disciples was increasing continually.

Since the apostles had no way of knowing every individual among the brethren, they entrusted the other

THE MISSION OF THE DEACON

believers to help them. This is revealed throughout this account. Let us look again at our verses from Acts 6.

> *Then the twelve called the MULTITUDE OF THE DISCIPLES unto them, and said, It is not reason that we should leave the word of God, and serve tables. Wherefore, brethren, LOOK YE OUT among you seven men of honest report, full of the Holy Ghost and wisdom, whom we may appoint over this business. But we will give ourselves continually to prayer, and to the*

THE MISSION OF THE DEACON

ministry of the word. And the saying pleased the WHOLE MULTITUDE and THEY CHOSE... (Acts 6:2-5 Emphasis Mine)

The apostles received helped from the brethren since those chosen would serve among them. The procedure then was uncomplicated – look for men who had already proven themselves spiritually mature and willing servants. Your call to serve will be affirmed by others in the Church.

Make sure that your desire to serve is accompanied by a call to serve. Though

THE MISSION OF THE DEACON

the brethren chose the men, the final ordination of these men were left up to leadership.

Understand that these events recorded in Acts paved the way for the development of the deacon's office. Comprehension of the circumstances surrounding these first servants gives a clear foundation for the operation and purpose of the Deacon's Office in the Church.

Before going to the next section, remember your call to service is one of great importance. It not only helps meet

THE MISSION OF THE DEACON

the needs of others, but it frees others to do the work of the ministry.

THE MISSION OF THE DEACON

THE MISSION OF THE DEACON

Questions for Review:

1) What was the original problem that led to a quest for servants?

2) What were the apostles' reasons for appointing servants?

3) What was the initial procedure used to appoint servants?

Notes:

THE MISSION OF THE DEACON

THE MISSION OF THE DEACON

-Section 2-

The Qualifications of Servants

THE MISSION OF THE DEACON

THE MISSION OF THE DEACON

The apostles proposed a solution to their problem. Find individuals whom they could appoint to ensure that a particular segment of the widows was not neglected in the food distribution. However, in chapter one, accompanying the request for servants was a standard by which these servants were to be chosen.

In this section, we will discuss the qualifications for servants. Regardless of the type of service, you perform in the Church (though these things specifically refer to deacons); you must have these same qualifications if you

THE MISSION OF THE DEACON

desire effectiveness.

Wherefore, brethren, look ye out among you seven men of honest report, full of the Holy Ghost and wisdom, whom we may appoint over this business. (Acts 6:3 KJV)

The apostles listed three qualifications that the chosen servants should possess. From these verses, we discover (what I have termed) the holy trinity of servant hood.

Anyone who serves and has a desire to serve in the Church should have these qualities. Moreover, anyone set apart to

THE MISSION OF THE DEACON

the Deacon's ministry should have these traits also. Consider these as you prepare for service.

Qualification of Honest Report

The first qualification listed is that of an "honest report." In simple terms, this refers to the reputation of those selected. It is important that anyone who is called to serve have a solid reputation among those who are served. This enhances the servant's ability to minister effectively without rejection and undue criticism.

When you enter into any form of Christian service, make sure that you are

THE MISSION OF THE DEACON

known for your godly character and manner. This is especially important for deacons. As you serve, eyes will not only be upon your works, but upon your character.

It is interesting to note that the apostles mentioned character before anointing in choosing servants. This reveals that the foundation for effective service is an individual's character and not the anointing or wisdom an individual possesses.

Since character is important to your walk with Christ and your service in the

THE MISSION OF THE DEACON

kingdom of God, it has to be monitored and developed daily. A servant in the Church is first a servant of Christ. Therefore, your service has to be governed by the desire to please Christ, which is revealed in becoming more like Him.

When examining your maturity and growth, look to the standards set by Christ. In the well-known list in Galatians of the fruit of the Spirit, we discover the necessary character traits for those who serve, especially deacons.

1) Love – Those who serve have to full of by compassion. God is love. His service

THE MISSION OF THE DEACON

must be done through love for Him and His people. (I John 4:8)

2) Joy – You must serve possessing happiness with contentment. This will bring stability when you are mistreated or experiencing hard times while serving. The Kingdom of God is not meat and drink, but righteousness, JOY, and peace in the Holy Ghost. (Romans 14:17)

3) Peace – The servant has to seek for peace and let God's peace dwell in him in adverse situations. (John 14:27)

4) Patience – As you serve, you need to be able to endure and wait on God. In

THE MISSION OF THE DEACON

addition, you will need to exercise patience as you interact with others in service. (Isaiah 40:31)

5) Kindness – The servant cannot be biased or partial, but be kind to all, displaying the love of the Father. He is our ultimate example of kindness. (Luke 6: 35)

6) Goodness – The servant has to do good unto all men, in spite of their actions, in and outside of the Church. (Galatians 6:10)

7) Faithfulness – Servants have to maintain their faith in God, but God also

must find them faithful to whatever tasks are before them. (I Corinthians 4:2)

8) Gentleness – Servants, especially deacons, must not deal with people out of a harsh spirit, but from one of care and concern. (Galatians 6:1)

9) Self-Control – Servants must practice self-control when it comes to the flesh, but also in their dealings with others. (James 3:2)

If you possess these qualities, you will not fail in your Christian service, or in any assignment that is given to you by leadership. Character ensures that you will have an honest report among those in the Church.

Qualification of Full of the Holy Ghost

After the apostles mentioned the need for the chosen servants to have a good reputation, they said that they should also be full of the Holy Ghost. Remember, they were choosing men to serve food.

But, they did not want men serving, even in food distribution, without the Holy Ghost. They not only needed to be saved, but they needed to be FULL of the Holy Ghost.

THE MISSION OF THE DEACON

In the Church, no one should perform any type of service among Christians without being full of the Holy Ghost. As you enter into your place in service, endeavor to remain full of the Holy Ghost.

The Holy Spirit has to be active in your life in Christian service. Deacons need to be full of the Holy Ghost to effectively perform their duties.

Before moving on to the last qualification, we want to look at two aspects of being full of the Holy Ghost.

THE MISSION OF THE DEACON

Spirit-filled Living

Outside of service, every Christian has to be filled with the Holy Spirit. This is the first aspect of His infilling. The Holy Spirit has to be the governing force in the believer's life, which is manifested in holy living and conduct. Paul refers to this aspect of the Spirit's indwelling,

> *And be not drunk with wine, wherein is excess; but be filled with the Spirit. (Eph 5:18 KJV)*

As Paul wrote to the Ephesians to be aware of the time that they are living in, he urged them to walk carefully. They

THE MISSION OF THE DEACON

were not to live ungodly and loose. They were to reveal the light of Christ in their daily lives. To substantiate his statements, Paul tells them that they were to be filled with the Spirit.

In this instance, it was not for Christian service, but for righteous living and manner. Servants in the Church verify their call to serve by their godly conduct, which is a reflection of the Spirit's filling.

Spirit-filled Service

Servants, especially deacons, also need the power of the Holy Ghost to be active in their lives for Christian service.

THE MISSION OF THE DEACON

This is the second aspect of the filling of the Holy Ghost. One needs character and power to serve. Those who serve need the empowering work of the Holy Spirit to be in their lives or their service will not be effective. Consider the following:

> *And when they had prayed, the place was shaken where they were assembled together; and they were all filled with the Holy Ghost, and they spake the word of God with boldness. (Acts 4:31 KJV)*

After Peter and John were beaten for their ministry, they came back to the assembly of the saints. We find that after they had prayed, they were FILLED with the Holy Ghost and began to speak God's word with boldness.

In this instance, we find that the Holy Ghost filled them in order for them to continue ministry. As a deacon or servant, you have to continually seek out His presence that you will be able to perform your duties effectively and boldly.

Remember, your appointment and call to serve is an admonition also to be filled with the Holy Ghost. Those whom the apostles appointed to serve food needed this qualification and you need it also.

Qualification of Full of Wisdom

The final qualification outlined by the apostles is that of wisdom. Wisdom is needed to handle challenging situations and difficult people.

The selected servants would need wisdom, even in food distribution. Any situation involving more than one person will bring conflict; wisdom is needed to handle them.

Consider the words of James:

THE MISSION OF THE DEACON

But the wisdom that is from above is first pure, then peaceable, gentle, and easy to be entreated, full of mercy and good fruits, without partiality, and without hypocrisy. (James 3:17 KJV)

Deacons need to be full of wisdom in their service in the Church. They need wisdom to employ the directives of leadership as well as interact with others.

Where there is wisdom, the following things should be present:

1. Peace – James stated that godly wisdom is peaceable. It comes in peace

THE MISSION OF THE DEACON

and it produces peace in the situation. Your service should bring peace in the Church.

2. Gentle – When wisdom is present, you will operate in the nature of Christ. You will not be offensive in manner or dispensing of duties.

3. Easy Entreatment – Wisdom will cause you not to be stubborn. People should find it easy to approach you, even when there is conflicting opinions concerning a situation.

4. Mercy and Good Fruits – Wisdom will cause you to be merciful to others when

they are in error or need restoration. Your interaction with others, through wisdom, should produce good fruits in the lives of others.

5. No Partiality – Deacons and others who serve should never do so "playing favorites." When wisdom is present, it will cause an individual to be objective and fair in their dealings with others.

6. No Hypocrisy – In this instance, hypocrisy is referring to division. When one operates in the wisdom of God, it should not divide the Church or its members, but rather promote unity and

THE MISSION OF THE DEACON

solidarity among the people.

We understand that the apostles looked for qualified servants, even to distribute food. Deacons and those who serve need the same qualifications today. Remember that you are called to serve God's people. Thus, it must be done with His character and nature and in subjection to leadership.

In our next section, we will explore, in detail, the results of these servants being appointed. The same results should be realized as the deacon ministers within the Church.

THE MISSION OF THE DEACON

Questions for Review:

1) What are the three qualifications needed for Christian service?

2) Explain the qualification of an "honest report.

3) Explain the two-fold way an individual experiences the Spirit's filling.

Notes:

THE MISSION OF THE DEACON

THE MISSION OF THE DEACON

-Section 3-

The Quality of Service

THE MISSION OF THE DEACON

In the first two sections, we discussed the quest and qualifications of servants. However, the servants were chosen to fulfill a need. Only in accomplishing the task for which they were appointed.

In this section, we want to discuss the quality of the service that the seven men demonstrated. As deacons and servants in the Church, your service should produce the same level of quality.

In the business world, certain industries have quality assurance inspectors. They make sure that the product or service is top quality.

THE MISSION OF THE DEACON

We want to present three quality assurance tests that each servant has to look for in their service. Continuing our examination of Acts 6, we discover three products of effective service.

Mortification of Murmuring

In our first section, we discovered that a problem arose in the early Church. Some of the widows were overlooked in the daily food distribution. As a result, people were complaining, which we know will lead to division.

And in those days, when the number of the disciples was multiplied, there

THE MISSION OF THE DEACON

arose a murmuring of the Grecians against the Hebrews, because their widows were neglected in the daily ministration. (Acts 6:1 KJV)

The apostles appointed servants to bring death to the complaining. You must also understand this verse in context. All of the believers up until this point were Jews. The scriptures, however, denote a distinction by calling one group Grecians and the other Hebrews.

The distinction was made because the Grecians were Jews who had allowed the Greek culture and language to

THE MISSION OF THE DEACON

influence their lives as opposed to the Hebrews who had remained faithful to their Jewish heritage and culture. Therefore, there was a division among those lines. Now, both sets of Jews were believers in Christ. So, the Grecian widows being neglected stirred up old prejudices between the people.

The men appointed to serve would need a good reputation so that they would not be accused of prejudice. They needed the Holy Ghost to empower them as they served. In addition, they needed the wisdom of God to execute their duty

THE MISSION OF THE DEACON

while squashing division and murmuring.

As a deacon ministers, his service should always be to uphold the unity of the assembly. When complaints and murmurings arise, it should be in his heart to kill it and not to flame it.

This is one sure way you can test your service – it should always result in the maintenance of unity and peace within the assembly of believers. Deacons should not allow anyone to divide the Church, defame leadership, or allow others to criticize and judge one another, but seek for peace and reconciliation in the Church.

THE MISSION OF THE DEACON

Magnification of the Word

At the end of Chapter 6, we see the results of the servants fulfilling their duty.

And the word of God increased. (Acts 6:7a KJV)

After the servants were put in place, Luke (the writer of Acts) records that the first outcome was that the word of God increased. The apostles, in the beginning, stated that it was time for them to give themselves over totally to the word of God and prayer.

Thus, after the contention arose in

THE MISSION OF THE DEACON

the assembly, they needed others to oversee and facilitate the daily food distribution. Here, we learn that their intent and goal was accomplished. The word of God increased; that is, it was magnified.

Deacons and servants are placed in positions of ministry and service so that leadership can focus on the presentation and propagation of the word of God. The men were needed to lift burdens from the apostles.

If a deacon is fulfilling his task, unnecessary tasks and burdens normally

THE MISSION OF THE DEACON

placed upon pastors and leaders are diminished. This should result in a greater revelation and presentation of the word of God from those in leadership.

This is accomplished because:

1) The pastor and leaders have more time for prayer and study.

2) The pastor and leaders are not overtaxed with ministry maintenance.

The deacon and servant's ministry should release leadership from undue concerns and tasks associated with the Church so that leadership can provide

THE MISSION OF THE DEACON

spiritual instruction and insight without hindrances. One fallacy in the Church is many tasks that can and should be done by others are often performed by the pastor and leadership.

Some think it is because of the mindset of members in the assembly. However, another cause of this is because those who should be performing these tasks did not have the same qualifications as these initial servants listed in Acts 6.

Again, it is imperative that as you prepare to serve as a deacon and in any other capacity that you have the necessary qualifications for service.

Multiplication of Disciples

The result of the servants being placed in fruitful service was that there was an increase in the number of disciples and priests who were obedient to the faith.

Once the apostles allowed these men to serve freely, the word of God increased and the number of disciples multiplied.

...and the number of the disciples multiplied in Jerusalem greatly; and a

THE MISSION OF THE DEACON

great company of the priests were obedient to the faith. (Acts 6:7 KJV)

The multiplication of disciples was due to the apostles' ministry of the word and due to the servants' ministering.

Since murmuring, contention, and division was silenced, the people were able to receive the word and grow thereby. The subsequent unity contributed to the others receiving the message presented by the apostles. Remember the words of Jesus,

By this shall all men know that ye are my disciples, if ye have love one to

THE MISSION OF THE DEACON

another. John 13:35 (KJV)

Those present in Jerusalem beheld the unity and love demonstrated among the people of God, which contributed to their identification with Christ.

In turn, many were able to embrace the message of Christ. In addition to the number of disciples multiplying, the number of priests who became obedient to the faith increased accordingly.

The preaching of the word combine with increased unity resulted in priests obeying the call to faith in Jesus Christ. When deacons and servants fulfill their

THE MISSION OF THE DEACON

roles according to the will of God, there will be an increase in those who receive the gospel.

Now, we will look more closely at the deacon's ministry and qualifications, which are specific to those who are appointed to this office.

THE MISSION OF THE DEACON

THE MISSION OF THE DEACON

Questions for Review:

1) What are the three results of a fruitful deacon and servant's ministry?

2) What can you do to ensure that your service is fruitful and effective?

3) How are pastors and leaders freed through the deacon and servant's ministry?

THE MISSION OF THE DEACON

THE MISSION OF THE DEACON

Notes:

THE MISSION OF THE DEACON

-Section 4-

The Office of the Deacon

THE MISSION OF THE DEACON

THE MISSION OF THE DEACON

In the first sections, we discussed servant hood in the Church, which includes the deacon's ministry. The quest for servants, again, forms the foundation for the development of the deacon's ministry in the Church. Now, we will look specifically at the deacon's office.

As we consider this office, we want to keep some foundational truths in mind. First, the Greek word for deacon is diakonos, which has several implications and uses. Its primary meaning is servant.

Diakonos is derived from an old Greek term which means to run errands.

THE MISSION OF THE DEACON

Also, it is used to refer to attendants and waiters. It is used to denote service. Hence, a deacon is primarily a servant and attendant in the Church.

Though this ministry is rooted is service, its foundation is in the spiritual character and conduct of the one who occupies this office. With this in mind, we will now look at the deacon's character.

> *Likewise must the deacons be grave, not doubletongued, not given to much wine, not greedy of filthy lucre.*
> *1 Tim 3:8 (KJV)*

THE MISSION OF THE DEACON

The Deacon's Character

To begin his directives for the placement of individuals into the deacon's office, Paul lists certain character traits for the deacon. Remember, your qualification as a deacon rests in your character and not your career.

You may have abilities and knowledge, but they are of no use to the Church if they are not tempered with godly character.

The Deacon is Honorable

The first character trait that Paul

THE MISSION OF THE DEACON

gives for the deacon is grave. It comes from a Greek term, which means honorable or honest. In order to effectively serve as a deacon, you must be able to tell the truth in every circumstance and situation.

From the examination of the first servants, we discover that a deacon then will act as a liaison between the people and those in leadership.

To do this effectively, the deacon has to be honorable and not biased in decision making as well as reporting issues, which may arise in the Church.

THE MISSION OF THE DEACON

The deacon has to be able to speak the truth in love. He must have an honorable reputation among the people so that his decisions can be received without substantial suspicion.

To remain honorable, the deacon must do 2 things according to the scriptures.

Have no respect of persons. The deacon who only stands for Christ and the welfare of the assembly will not be tempted to operate without integrity.

My brethren, have not the faith of our Lord Jesus Christ, the Lord of

THE MISSION OF THE DEACON

glory, with respect of persons. James 2:1 (KJV)

He will represent God by not having a respect of persons as he executes his duties in accordance with established leadership.

Have genuine love. The deacon is to have sincere and genuine love for the Church. He has to love the Church as Christ does.

Seeing ye have purified your souls in obeying the truth through the Spirit unto unfeigned love of the brethren, see that ye love one another with a pure heart fervently. 1 Peter 1:22 (KJV)

In doing so, his service will always be rendered through the proper motivation. He will operate in a manner, which is consistent with the Christian faith.

The Deacon is Truthful

Continuing his prescriptive for the deacon's character, Paul states that the deacon must not be double-tongued. The Greek term for this word is *dilogos*. Literally, it means two worded. Paul, then, is exhorting deacons to be honest and truthful. They must be able to report what has happened and what is said clearly and accurately. They should only hear and report one story, not two different versions.

> *But speaking the truth in love, may grow up into him in all things, which is the head, even Christ. Eph 4:15 (KJV)*

Quite simply, the deacon has to tell the truth all time, regardless of the situation and who is involved. People should be able to trust the words that come from them. Many times, the deacon reports what the leadership is saying to

THE MISSION OF THE DEACON

the people.

In addition, the deacon brings back the issues of the people to leadership. Hence, a deacon who is double tongued (switching the story, exaggerating, and the like) will be a destructive force rather than a constructive influence.

The Deacon is Sober

The next character trait, if you will, that Paul lists is sobriety. He states that the deacon is not to be a drunkard or given to much wine. This is a clear call to a deacon's sobriety. The deacon must remember Paul's exhortation to the

Ephesians.

> *And be not drunk with wine, wherein is excess; but be filled with the Spirit. Eph 5:18 (KJV)*

The deacon is not to be under the influence of alcohol. This exhortation also applies to today's legal and illegal substances that could affect the deacon's sobriety, which will affect his service.

In other words, deacons should not be drunkards or drug addicts. The controlling force in their lives should be the Holy Spirit.

THE MISSION OF THE DEACON

The Deacon is Noble in Business

The final character trait, in particular, that Paul lists for the deacon is that he is not to be greedy for filthy lucre. He is not to be after money regardless of how he gets it.

This means he should not be crooked in personal and Church business affairs. He should not be a gambler (of any kind).

For the love of money is the root of all evil: which while some coveted after, they have erred from the faith, and pierced themselves through with

THE MISSION OF THE DEACON

many sorrows. 1 Tim 6:10 (KJV)

Moreover, the deacon is not to treat the Church's finances like his own. If the deacon is involved with the finances, he should do it as a faithful steward and not a miserly tyrant. His stewardship within the Church's finances should be characterized by wisdom, honesty, and integrity.

The Deacon's Charge

After enumerating the necessary character traits for the deacon, Paul gives a three-fold charge to the deacon in the discharging of his duties.

THE MISSION OF THE DEACON

Holding the mystery of the faithfaith in a pure conscience. And let these also first be proved; then let them use the office of a deacon, being found blameless. 1 Tim 3:9-10 (KJV)

The deacon's character should be a clear reflection of the Christian faith. His motives and means for service ought to be pure bring honor to the Christian faith. In doing so, he will have a pure conscience as he operates in his office. This leads us to the first charge given to the deacon.

THE MISSION OF THE DEACON

Holding the Mystery of the Faith

A deacon must possess a clear knowledge and understanding of the doctrines of the Christian faith. Paul states that he should hold the mystery of the faith. This means that his knowledge should go beyond the superficial.

> *Study to shew thyself approved unto God, a workman that needeth not to be ashamed, rightly dividing the word of truth. 2 Tim 2:15 (KJV)*

He should be able to explain and expound upon the truths of the faith. The deacon should 0be a student of God's word in his personal life.

Having a Testimony above Reproach

A deacon has to maintain godly character before and after operating in this office. Hence, Paul states that let him first be proven. This simply means that his life should be examined. Some use this to justify ordination committees. They have their place.

However, what it implies is that based upon consistent observation of an individual's life, doctrine, and conduct, the decision to place them in the office should be based. Hence, the charge to the deacon

THE MISSION OF THE DEACON

is to maintain purity always and live a life that will be above reproach. He has to strive to remain blameless in all his affairs.

The deacon's testimony extends beyond his personal purity into the affairs of his home. Paul gives instructions concerning the deacon's wife and children.

Even so must their wives be grave, not slanderers, sober, faithful in all things. Let the deacons be the husbands of one wife, ruling their children and their own houses well.
1 Tim 3:11-12 (KJV)

All of these things factor into the deacon living above reproach, remaining blameless. He has to be able to lead his family in the faith; his wife demonstrating the same level of integrity and lifestyle as his own.

Make Full Use of the Office

All of Paul's statements lead to the final charge upon the deacon, make full use of the deacon's office.

> *For they that have used the office of a deacon well purchase to themselves a good degree, and great boldness in the faith which*

THE MISSION OF THE DEACON

is in Christ Jesus. 1 Tim 3:13 (KJV)

The deacon is expected to be faithful in his service. If his character and conduct are in order, he can use the office fully and be a great blessing to the Church.

In addition, he will be a true example of the Christian faith. To make full use of this office, the deacon must be faithful, committed, and dedicated to Christ, the Church, and the continuation of the Lord's work.

THE MISSION OF THE DEACON

Questions for Review:

1) Why is character important to the deacon's ministry?

2) What can you do to ensure that you have the proper character necessary to operate in the deacon's office?

3) Explain each of the 4 character traits listed by Paul necessary for a deacon.

4) Explain the deacon's charge.

Notes:

THE MISSION OF THE DEACON

THE MISSION OF THE DEACON

-Section 5-

The Deacon and the Church

THE MISSION OF THE DEACON

In the last section, we want to turn our attention to how the deacon should operate in the local Church. Since the deacon's ministry bridges the gap between leadership and the laity, it is imperative that the deacon executes his office with wisdom, grace, discretion, and humility in the fear of the Lord.

We want to look at three dynamics of the deacon's ministry within the local assembly. They are as follows:

1)   The Deacon and the Pastor

2)   The Deacon and the Laity

THE MISSION OF THE DEACON

3) The Deacon and the Deacons

The deacon has to know how to interact effectively and efficiently in the Church.

The Deacon and the Pastor

The deacon's relationship with the leadership has to be characterized by submission, obedience, and integrity. The deacon ministry is in place to relieve the burdens (of the pastor) that come with ministry. Hence, the deacon has to interact with the pastor in a respectable fashion. His service should not add to the pastor's labor, but alleviate it.

THE MISSION OF THE DEACON

Submission

The deacon has to have the heart of a servant governed by submission. He has to know how to submit to God, the pastor, and the needs of the local assembly.

Submitting yourselves one to another in the fear of God. Eph 5:21 (KJV)

Though the deacon will work with leadership in a very personal way, he has to remember that he is not there to lead the pastor, but be an extension of the pastor's ministry of service to the Church.

So, the deacon has to be clear as to what are the goals of the pastor and endeavor to see them implemented according to the will of God. This takes the spirit of submission. Without submission, a deacon can become a destructive force and a thorn in a pastor's side.

Obedience

The hallmark of the deacon's ministry is service. Effective service demands obedience. If a deacon is submitted to God and leadership, he will have no problem with obedience.

THE MISSION OF THE DEACON

Obey them that have the rule over you, and submit yourselves: for they watch for your souls, as they that must give account, that they may do it with joy, and not with grief: for that is unprofitable for you. Heb 13:17 (KJV)

A deacon cannot take his position for an excuse to enforce his own will and operate against established leadership and protocol. He must be in subjection to the pastor as others in the assembly.

Integrity

Integrity is important in the deacon's

interaction with the pastor. He must deal with the pastor with pure motives. He cannot use his office as an excuse to usurp the pastor's authority in the Church.

He should interact with the pastor in all honesty and without guile. He should not be a "smooth talker," but someone who represents the faith well.

> *For neither at any time used we flattering words, as ye know, nor a cloke of covetousness; God is witness. 1 Thess 2:5 (KJV)*

In addition, the deacon needs integrity so that he will not misrepresent

THE MISSION OF THE DEACON

God or the sentiments of the pastor as he interacts with the people. Moreover, the deacon should be trustworthy that the pastor can trust that whatever he gives him to do, it will be done without a hidden agenda or motive.

The Deacon and the Laity

The deacon's ministry is unique in that he is called to serve and lead concurrently. He has to be able to serve the pastor and the people, while being leaders (and examples) of the Christian faith to the people.

In the first sections, we saw that the

THE MISSION OF THE DEACON

installation of the servants had a direct influence upon the company of the disciples. The deacon must endeavor to have this same impact today.

He has to know how to interact among the people for their spiritual well-being. He has to know how to bring the people together for the cause of Christ and not fuel flames of division.

Since deacons are visible extension of the pastoral ministry, they need to care for the flock in the same manner as the pastor. Paul's description of the apostles' love and care for the church should mark

THE MISSION OF THE DEACON

the deacons' ministry.

> *Nor of men sought we glory, neither of you, nor yet of others, when we might have been burdensome, as the apostles of Christ. But we were gentle among you, even as a nurse cherisheth her children: So being affectionately desirous of you, we were willing to have imparted unto you, not the gospel of God only, but also our own souls, because ye were dear unto us. 1 Thess 2:6-8 (KJV)*

The deacon should not be after the glory of the men; more specifically, the

THE MISSION OF THE DEACON

laity. He should not serve so that he can be praised of men for his service. He has to remember that he lays up for himself treasure in heaven.

The deacon should not be burdensome to the pastor or church. He should not serve in expectation of some sort of visible gain, knowing that he shall receive of the Lord his just reward. Additionally, as the deacon operates in the church, he should be gentle.

The laity should not be afraid to approach a deacon nor be afraid of a deacon's potential response or his disposition. The deacon has to treat the laity as God's own children.

The Deacon and the Deacons

Finally, the deacons have to know how to interact with other deacons. They must not be in competition with one another. They have to endeavor to keep peace and unity among themselves as an example to others in the Church.

Paul's words to the Ephesians exemplify how the deacon is to interact with other deacons.

> *Let no corrupt communication proceed out of your mouth, but that*

THE MISSION OF THE DEACON

which is good to the use of edifying, that it may minister grace unto the hearers. And grieve not the holy Spirit of God, whereby ye are sealed unto the day of redemption. Let all bitterness, and wrath, and anger, and clamour, and evil speaking, be put away from you, with all malice: And be ye kind one to another, tenderhearted, forgiving one another, even as God for Christ's sake hath forgiven you. Eph 4:29-32 (KJV)

Deacons should know how to

THE MISSION OF THE DEACON

interact with one another. They should be men of character whose words will edify and not destroy one another. Deacons should respect one another as fellow laborers of the Lord. Because differences of opinions will arise, deacons have to know how to get over disputes and disagreements.

Meetings, discussions, and interactions should end in peace and forgiveness, not in bitterness and criticism. All this is done to ensure that the vision of the local church is accomplished, and the will of God fulfilled.

THE MISSION OF THE DEACON

The deacon who remembers that he is a servant of Christ, will not fail as he executes and operates in his office. Remember, the deacon who serves well will receive a great reward of the Christ.

THE MISSION OF THE DEACON

Questions for Review:

1) What three attributes should characterize the deacon's relationship with the pastor?

2) How should the deacon interact with the laity?

3) Describe the proper interaction between deacons.

Notes:

THE MISSION OF THE DEACON

BIBLIOGRAPHY

Lockman Foundation. *Comparative Study Bible.* Zondervan Publishing House. Grand Rapids, MI, c1984

Smith, William. *Smith's Bible Dictionary.* Holman Bible Publishers. Nashville, TN. c1994

The Bible Library. *The Bible Library CD Rom Disc.* Ellis Enterprises Incorporated, (c)1988 – 2000. 4205 McAuley Blvd., Suite 385,

Oklahoma City, OK 73120. All Rights Reserved.

THE MISSION OF THE DEACON

Notes:

_____

_____

_____

_____

_____

_____

_____

_____

THE MISSION OF THE DEACON

www.ingramcontent.com/pod-product-compliance
Lightning Source LLC
Chambersburg PA
CBHW050342010526
44119CB00049B/656